SPORTS ENCYCLOPEDIA

TARGET AND WATER SPORTS

Om Books International

Contents

Target Sports

Before man settled down to build civilisation, majority of human beings were hunter-gatherers. Sometimes, the hunters had to catch prey in a swift and elusive manner even from a far distance. Men would hurl rocks, sharp sticks or employ different instruments to facilitate this, which needed a strong aiming capability. This gave rise to the sport of hitting targets with various weapons.

Target sports are those which involve the aiming of a projectile weapon at a target. These sports are usually distinguished by various criteria such as the range at which the target is placed, the instrument used and the position of the shooter. As a result, target sports tend to have a variety of ranges. They are played in many different types of environments ranging from arenas to wooded playing fields. Target sports today are very mainstream and are included in most international sports meets.

Did you know? Many times, target sports are combined with various different types of skills such as moving and camouflage to simulate real-life combat environments. Laser tag and Paintball are two very common examples of such sports.

Archery

Stories of William Tell shooting an apple off his child's head, Robin Hood and prince Paris of Troy, which depict the art of archery, are very famous. Modern archery has evolved from the ancient martial art of the bow and arrow.

Origin

The origin of archery is dated back to the late Paleolithic era, around 10000–9000 BCE. The oldest evidence of archery in Europe comes from the Stellmoor in the Ahrensburg Valley of Hamburg, Germany. All of the classical civilisations have long traditions of archery in their armies.

The English proved the importance of archery through the famous English longbow. But, with the advent of gunpowder, the importance of archery went down greatly. 1840s saw the first attempt to turn archery into a modern sport by standardising the rules.

The World Archery Federation governs the target archery since 1930s. Archery was made a part of Paris Olympics, in 1900. Other forms, like field archery and cosplay, exist for amateurs.

Rules

Archery was dropped from the Olympics because there were no internationally recognised rules for it. Each Olympic archery event, from 1896 to 1920, followed a different set of rules. It was only in 1972 that archery was re-introduced as an individual event and in 1988, the team event was added to the Olympics.

In the Olympics, archery takes place at a standard range of 70 m. Competition is divided into "ends". An archer shoots three or six arrows per end, depending on the type of round. After each end, the competitors walk to the target to score and retrieve their arrows. An Olympic event makes use of 122 cm target faces.

An archer doing target-practice.

Working from the outside in, targets are coloured as follows:

- Rings one and two – white
- Rings three and four – black
- Rings five and six – blue
- Rings seven and eight – red
- Rings nine, ten and ten inner – gold

If an arrow touches a boundary, it is scored to the higher ring. The player with the highest score at the end of the match, wins.

Archers also have a time limit. They must go through an end of three arrows in two minutes.

The only type of bow allowed to be used at the Olympic level is the recurve bow.

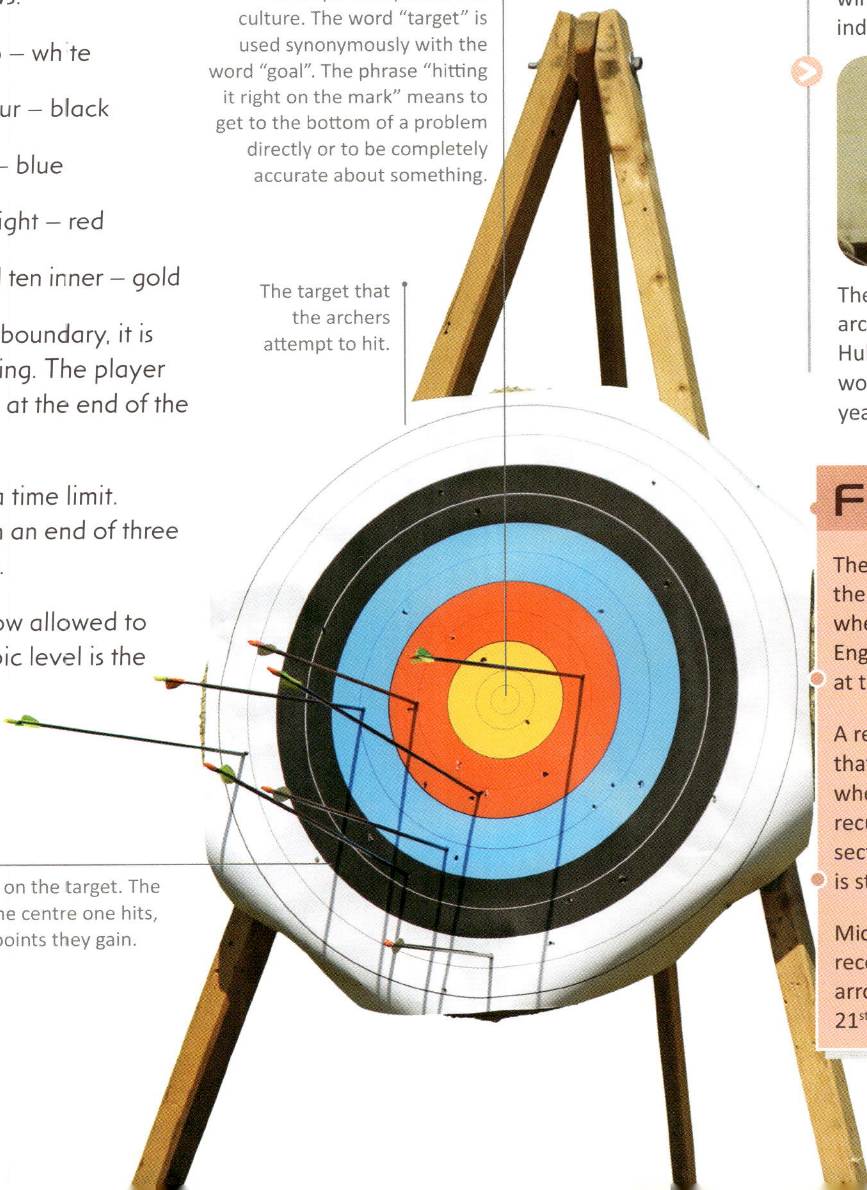

The target has actually become an important part of our culture. The word "target" is used synonymously with the word "goal". The phrase "hitting it right on the mark" means to get to the bottom of a problem directly or to be completely accurate about something.

The target that the archers attempt to hit.

The circles on the target. The closer to the centre one hits, the more points they gain.

Wall of fame

Kim Woo-jin is the winner of Olympic gold medal in 2024 individual event. He is also a three-time world champion in the men's individual recurve event at the World Archery Championships.

Lim Si-hyeon is a South Korean archer, achieved remarkable success at the 2024 Olympics, winning three gold medals in the individual team, and mixed events.

The best all-time performing archer at the Olympic games is Hubert Van Innis of Belgium, who won six gold medals between the years 1900 and 1920.

Fact card

The English longbow changed the course of European history when an outnumbered, underfed English force defeated the French at the battle of Agincourt.

A recurve bow is a bow with tips that curve away from the archer when the bow is strung. In a recurve bow, the string touches a section of the limb when the bow is strung.

Michele Frangilli is a world record holder for 25 m 60 arrows which he shot on 21st November, 2001.

Pitch and Putt

Clubs used to play pitch and putt.

Golf is a fairly complicated sport. As a result, many people liked the idea of golf, but found it too restrictive and expensive. Pitch and putt evolved from such an idea.

Origin

Pitch and putt is an amateur sport, which is very similar to golf, but much simplified. The exact origins of the game are very unclear. Generally, it is thought that people started playing golf with a fewer and fewer number of clubs.

The first instances of pitch and putt occurred in Ireland in the 1940s. This was either to cut down on expense or make the game simpler, or both. They also started selecting shorter distance holes to play golf on.

Pitch and putt is a well-regulated sport with different regulatory bodies. Today, pitch and putt is organised internationally by the European Pitch and Putt Association since 1999, by the International Pitch and Putt Federation since 2006 and by the International Pitch and Putt Association since 2009.

For all these advantages, pitch and putt has its own handicap system and applies the rules of FIPPA/IPPA with exceptions, which are specifically approved in each country.

A club used for playing pitch and putt is usually made of stainless steel and is made so that it is easy to swing.

A player estimates the distance and the direction of the ball.

Green flat lands on which the game can be played.

A metal flag indicates the number of the hole.

Fact card

- The Federation of International Pitch and Putt Associations (FIPPA) stages a biennial pitch and putt world cup. Since 2009, they also have a world stroke play championship. These are the two most important tournaments of the sport.

Rules

In pitch and putt, a hole length is typically limited to 70 m or 80 yards. The other rules are almost similar to those of golf, with a few exceptions.

For international competitions:

- the length of the hole is limited to 70 m
- the length of the course is limited to 1,000 m
- players may use a putter and only one other club

The game is played from artificially raised teeing surfaces, using a tee.

As compared to golf, pitch and putt also makes use of 18 holes. However, unlike golf that has 72, pitch and putt has only 54 pars. Where an entire game of golf can take from four to five hours, pitch and putt takes only about an hour to an hour and a half. The golf championship course is about 150 acres, whereas pitch and putt needs only 15.

Woodball

Woodball is a garden game, which is a mix of croquet, golf and other such sports. It is now played on different terrains.

Origin

Ming-Hui Weng invented woodball in 1990. According to the official International Woodball Federation site, it happened as follows:

"He just wanted to build a garden for his father to take a walk and enjoy the beautiful view, in the scenic spot of Nei-Shuang-His, situated in Shih-lin, Taipei City. After mowing the weeds of the hillside, he found that there were terraced fields, which could be developed as an outdoor exercise place."

As a result, woodball was developed as an inexpensive sport that could be played in a small area without the ball being lost.

The ball has to pass through a woodball gate.

Rules

Woodball is played either individually or in teams. The players use the mallet provided to knock a ball through the gates on the course. The game is analogous to golf. The objective is to get the ball through as many gates as possible in the fewest number of strokes.

Regarding boundaries or balls passing or not passing through fully, the rules of golf apply.

The game is played on grass, sand or turf. Instead of using a hole to complete the strokes as in golf, woodball uses a gate, which is a very small soccer goalpost.

The sport of woodball has been made a part of the Asian Beach Games, in 2008.

A wooden mallet is used to hit the ball through the post on the field.

The game is played with the wooden ball.

The player grips the handle of the mallet to play.

The head of the mallet is used to hit the ball.

Woodball is a part of the Asian Beach Games (ABG), which is a multi-sport event. These events are held every two years. The first ever Asian Beach Games were held in Bali, Indonesia, in 2008. The games are regulated by the Olympic Council of Asia. Currently, Thailand is the champion of these games, closely followed by China and then Indonesia.

Fact card

- The IWbF is located in Taipei, Taiwan.
- It consists of national teams from 44 countries.

Trugo

The game of trugo or "TruGo" evolved in Australia. It was invented by railway workers, who used the tools at hand for recreation.

Origin

Railway workers in the 1920s invented trugo in the Newport Railway Workshops, in the Western suburbs of Melbourne. The first club was in the suburb of Yarraville, Victoria. The requirements for the sport were based on what the railway workers could find:

1. A pitch as long as a carriage
2. A goalpost as wide as the space between two seats
3. A sledgehammer to be used as a mallet
4. The internal component of buffers, that were the black rings

The game was played not unlike lawn bowls. It was played on the lawns outdoors.

A sledgehammer was used as a mallet by railway workers to play Trugo.

The game was played with the help of a mallet, which was used to strike the rubber ring. The objective of the game was to get the rubber ring to pass through the goalpost.

Gameplay

The objective of trugo is to score goals or points by striking a rubber ring (wheel) with a mallet through a pair of goal posts.

The player stands on a rubber mat and faces away from the goals, keeping the feet on either side of the wheel. The short handled mallet is swung between the player's legs to strike the wheel (similar to a game of "tunnel ball").

After four wheels have been struck, the players swap. A match is 24 shots long, 12 from each end. The team with the highest number of goals is declared winner at the end. The women's version of the game has the mallet being swept from the side, instead of between the legs. This game is popularly known as "GoTru".

Fact card

- People below the age of 65 were banned from playing in the league until the 1990s.
- Anthony Bourdain featured trugo on his travel show "No Reservations", in 2009.

A wooden mallet is used to play a game of Trugo.

The players have to pass these wheels through the goalposts.

Horseshoes

There is a popular saying, "close only counts in horseshoes and hand grenades". This jocularly reflects the fact that coming close to doing something rarely means anything; except in the game of horseshoes. This peculiar game involves throwing horseshoes at a stake and trying to snare it.

A player throws a horseshoe at a stake.

Origin

Horseshoes may have been developed from the Roman game of quoits. Quoits involve tossing iron rings onto a stake and trying to snare them on it. Roman officers occupying Britain from the first to the fifth century BCE may have spread it there.

However, there is no evidence regarding the existence of U-shaped horseshoes at that time. It is believed that peasants in Medieval Britain also adapted horseshoes to improvise the game of quoits. In colonial times, English settlers introduced the sport into North America.

Rules

The horseshoes are pitched at an inclined stake while standing within a box, which is 12 m away. Professional games continue till a score of 50 is reached, whereas the amateur ones stop at 21. Scoring is done in the following manner:

1 If the shoe is six inches or closer to the stake, one point is awarded for each shoe being closer than the opponent's.

2 Three points are awarded for each ringer.

3 If the shoes are equally distant or if the opponents have the same number of ringers, then it's considered a tie and none of the players scores.

These rules were devised and enforced by the NHPA (National Horseshoe Pitching Association) in USA and Canada.

An inning consists of one player pitching both the shoes in succession to one pit, followed by the other player. Only one player can score points at a given inning.

The game is usually played in sand or loose soil, where the stake can be dug into the ground and taken off conveniently.

A stake is pitched in the ground that the players aim for. This is also made from a heavy metal like iron or lead.

An iron horseshoe used to play the game is now replaced with smaller u-shaped metallic bits.

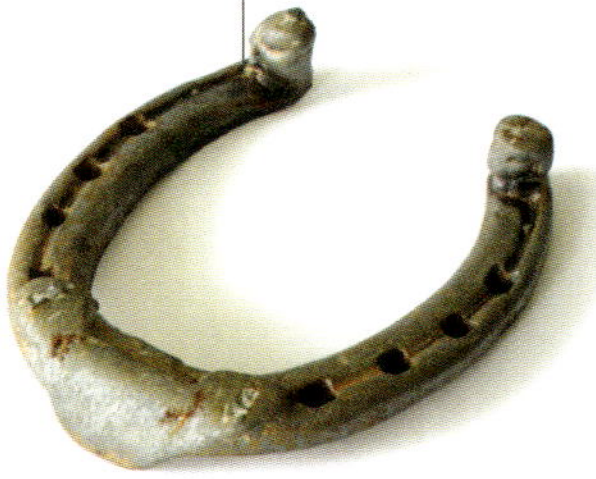

Fact card

- The shoes used today are not actual horseshoes but u-shaped pieces of metal, about twice the size.

Shooting

A group of female contestants pose with their guns.

The invention of gunpowder was one of the revolutionary developments that changed the face of warfare. Slowly, showing skill in firearms became important, which eventually turned into a sport. Shooting is a sport that involves hitting a target with a projectile weapon that shoots out slugs of metal.

Origin

Long before the advent of firearms, shooting as a test of skill began with archery. However, because of the lack of records regarding the origin and early use of firearms, it is not clear as to when exactly the instance of target shooting began. The earliest recorded shooting match was one held in Eichstäat, Bavaria, in 1477. The shooters competed at a 200 m (220 yards) match and used matchlock rifles.

It was only with the rise of clubs like the National Rifle Association (NRAs) of Great Britain and the USA that shooting as a game started becoming popular. By 1903, the NRA began to establish rifle clubs in all major colleges, universities and military academies. French pistol champion and the founder of the modern Olympics, Pierre de Coubertin participated in many of these early competitions. This is probably why, there was the inclusion of five shooting events in the 1896 Olympics.

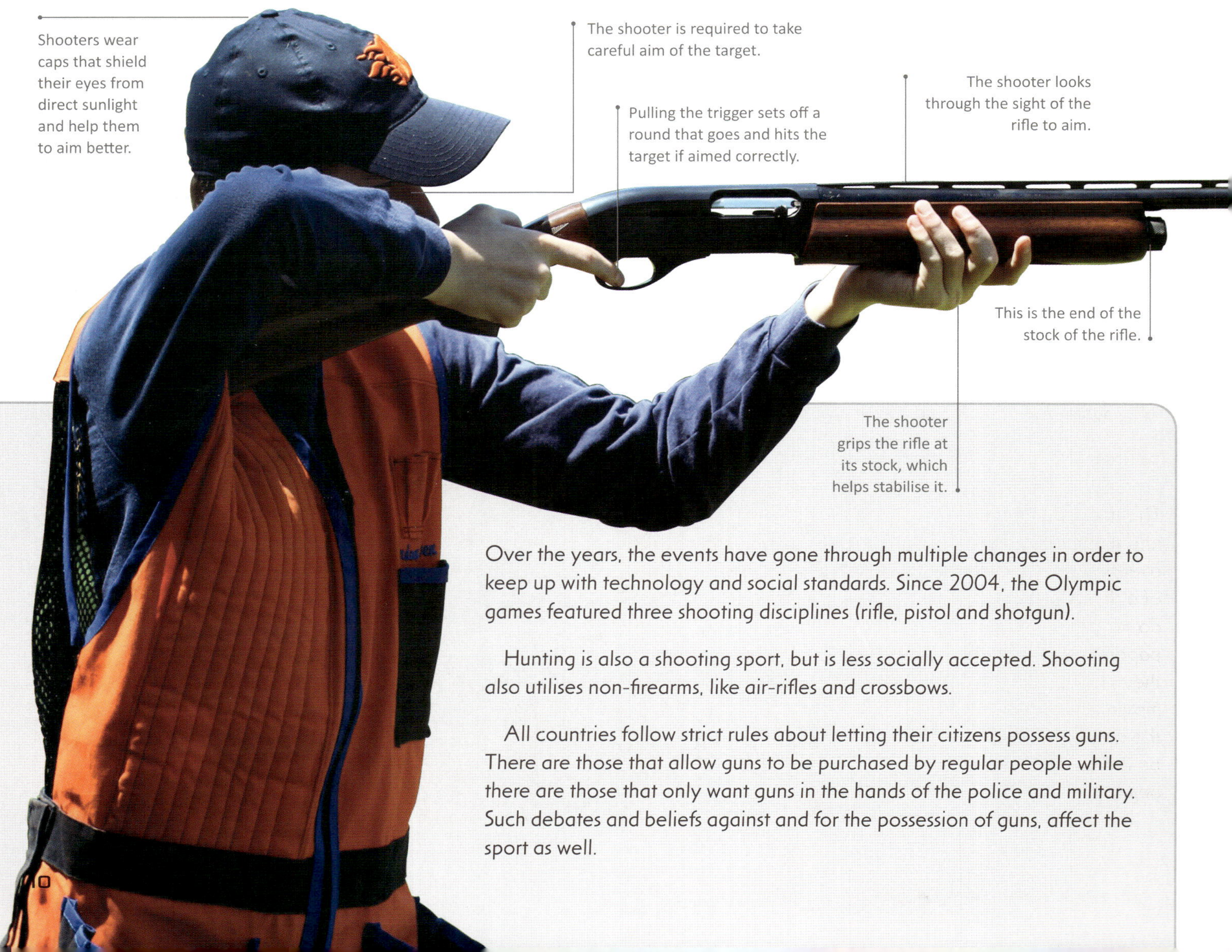

Over the years, the events have gone through multiple changes in order to keep up with technology and social standards. Since 2004, the Olympic games featured three shooting disciplines (rifle, pistol and shotgun).

Hunting is also a shooting sport, but is less socially accepted. Shooting also utilises non-firearms, like air-rifles and crossbows.

All countries follow strict rules about letting their citizens possess guns. There are those that allow guns to be purchased by regular people while there are those that only want guns in the hands of the police and military. Such debates and beliefs against and for the possession of guns, affect the sport as well.

Rules

All world championships are regulated by the International Shooting Union, formed in 1907. As of 1998, it is known as the International Shooting Sport Federation (ISSF)

Paper targets are used in shooting, with sizes varying from sport to sport. Each target has a number of concentric circles marked from one to 10 in an outward direction. Each match has a specific number of rounds to be fired. The player with the highest score at the end is declared the winner.

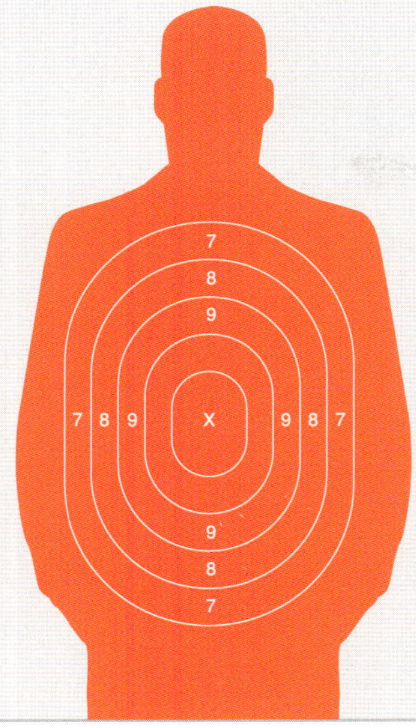

A player waits to receive a new set of bullets to refill his rifle.

Based on the factors, like the type of firearms used, the nature of the target, etc., the shooting technique differs. The position of the player and his/her breathing play an important role while handling a firearm.

Shooting occurs in multiple disciplines.
The ones currently on the Olympics schedule are:

- Air pistol
- Air rifle
- Double trap
- Trap
- Skeet
- Rapid fire pistol
- Rifle prone
- Rifle three positions

The trap, double trap and skeet are shotgun events. Due to the nature of a shotgun, shooters do not attempt to aim at paper targets. Instead, they attempt to shoot fast moving clay "birds" out of the air. The score is based on the number of birds being shot.

Players use one eye to hold an aim to avoid parallax.

The sight of the gun has a lens that gives a clear view of the target.

Players wear a glove that helps to grip the gun so that it doesn't slip when the fire is shot.

Wall of fame

American player Kimberly "Kim" Rhode is a six-time Olympic medal winner in double trap and skeet shooting.

Indian shooter Abhinav Bindra is a world and Olympic champion in the 10 m air rifle category.

The best all-time performing shooter at the Olympic games is Carl Osburn from the USA. He won 11 medals between 1912-1924.

Fact card

- Shooting as a sport didn't really develop until the nineteenth century because back then, the firearms produced were too inaccurate for competitions.
- Earlier, targets were shaped like humans or animals but that was discontinued to decrease the propagation of shooting as a violent sport.
- The 1900 Olympics had hunting as a sport, where live pigeons were used as targets.

Darts

People throwing little darts at a dartboard is an iconic group activity while hanging out and relaxing. So, it might be a little surprising to know that today, darts are one of the extremely competitive and rigorous sports.

Origin

Darts were historically used in warfare; skirmishers used hand-thrown darts of varying sizes. These were similar to miniature javelins or blowpipe darts.

Throwing darts was a training game for the English archers. The game was also popular with Tudor monarchs, starting from Henry VIII. As a sport, darts has evolved from this practice.

The sport of throwing darts is regulated by the World Darts Federation, which has over 500,000 members across 50 different countries.

Winmau world masters, the WDF world cup and the embassy world professional darts championship are some of the major championships of this game.

The manufacturers of dart boards use bright colours in the point scoring area as this minimises the shadows of the thrown darts. The colours and illuminations used should be able to resist accidental piercing. These illuminations should otherwise be kept away from the hitting area of the board. This is called "dartboard illumination".

A dartboard is marked with numbers to award points to the player whose dart lands in that area.

A metal dart is aimed and thrown at a dartboard to score.

The inner bullseye is worth 50 points.

Fact card

Dartboards are made of sisal fibres bound together. Because of the material, the dart sticking on the board causes no permanent damage.

The purpose of the flights is to prevent the rear of the dart from overtaking the front.

Rules

The board is divided into 20 sectors, valued from one to 20. Six rings determine the scoring:

- An inner bullseye worth 50 points.
- An outer bullseye worth 25 points.
- A wide single-scoring ring.
- A narrow triple-scoring ring.
- Another wide single-scoring ring.
- Outermost, a narrow double-scoring ring.

Throws must be made from 2.37 m away, which sometimes may range up to 3 m in some competitions. The centre of the board must be 1.73 m above the floor.

There are multiple variations of the game, like cricket, football, round the clock and so on.

Croquet

The game of croquet involves a mallet and a ball. The objective is to get the ball through the "hoops", with the help of the mallet. Croquet is usually played in a lawn and hence is also known as lawn croquet.

The mallet and the ball are used to play croquet.

Origin

Croquet, as a game, evolved from "paille-maille" (French for "pall-mall") played in France as early as the thirteenth century. It was introduced into England in the sixteenth century. Croquet combined the basic elements of paille-maille (running a mallet-driven ball through a hoop or hoops, to touch a peg as a goal) into a more complicated sport. It involves a series of six or more hoops, laid out in a specific pattern.

Croquet became highly popular as a social pastime in England during the 1860s. By the late 1870s, croquet had been eclipsed by another fashionable game, tennis. Many clubs, including the one at Wimbledon, converted their lawns to tennis courts.

There was a revival of the game in the 1890s, but croquet was always a minority sport. National individual participation never exceeds a few thousand players.

Croquet is played mostly on green lawns.

A hoop is made in the ground through which the player has to hit the ball.

Rules

Association croquet is the game which is played at an international level. It involves four balls, teamed in pairs. Both balls must go through every hoop for one pair to win.

The game's distinguishing feature is the "croquet shot". A croquet shot is when certain balls hit other balls and extra shots are allowed. The six hoops are arranged in such a manner that three hoops are at each end of the court with a centre peg.

One side takes the black and blue balls, the other takes red and yellow. Players can choose their colours at the start of the turn. The player then plays a stroke. If the player either hits the ball through the correct hoop ("runs" the hoop) or hits another ball (a "roquet"), the turn continues.

The player picks up his/her own ball after a roquet and puts it down next to the ball that it hit. The next shot is played with the "croquet stroke".

This game can also be played with your back to the hoops and hitting the ball with the mallet in between your legs. Another way is to brace the ball with the tip of your toe and hit it.

Fact card

- Different variations of croquet include garden croquet, golf croquet and roque. The last one is played with walls and on a clay surface.

Snooker

Snooker is one of the most complicated variations of billiards. It involves a large number of balls, and is played on a traditional billiards table. The objective of the players is to pocket the red and coloured balls in the correct order.

The chalk is rubbed at the tip of the cue stick to provide traction.

Origin

Billiards was a popular activity amongst the British Army officers stationed in India. However, snooker in its modern form originated only in the later half of the nineteenth century, when devising variations of the more traditional billiard games were attempted.

A variation devised in Jabalpur around 1875 added coloured balls to the traditional red and black. Sir Neville Chamberlain is credited for coming up with the final rules of modern snooker.

The game of snooker has grown since the early part of the twentieth century. Joe Davis, a professional billiards and snooker player, organised the first world snooker championship in 1927.

Colour television led to a massive boost in snooker's viewership and soon, it became an international sport.

The time it takes to complete a game or from the time when the first ball is hit to the time the last ball is potted, is called a "frame".

A snooker match has a predetermined number of frames, and the player winning the maximum frames wins the match. Usually, most of the professional matches need a player to win five frames.

The total number of successive points (excluding the foul points) that a player scores during one visit to the table is known as a "break". The highest possible break that a player can score is a 155 break, which is known as a "super maximum".

The player uses his dominant hand to grip the cue stick and control it to hit the cue ball.

The game needs not only a good aim but also strategising the positions of the ball on the table.

The cue stick is the only item in the entire game that is allowed to touch the cue ball during the game.

The other hand is used to support the front of the cue stick and take proper aim.

This white ball is a cue ball. It must be used to pocket any other coloured balls.

The pockets of the billiards table are at the corners and halfway down its lengths.

These are the coloured balls with which the game is played using a cue stick.

This is the green cloth of the table. It is rough and grips the balls very well.

All the balls on the table have to be arranged in a triangle at this semicircle, at the beginning of the game.

This is the edge of the table. The player may take its support to aim a shot.

Rules

The game is played with 22 balls:

- One white ball (the cue ball)
- 15 red balls
- Six numbered coloured balls including one yellow (valued at two points), one green (valued at three points), one brown (valued at four points), one blue (valued at five points), one pink (valued at six points) and one black (valued at seven points).

The green cloth of table has a directional nap running from the table's baulk end to the end spot of the black ball. That nap affects the movement of the cue ball, which depends on the direction of the cue ball being shot. It also depends on the spin of the ball.

The tip of the cue stick, made of wood or fibreglass, is used to strike the cue ball. The stick usually has a leather tip. The tip of the stick is "chalked" to ensure a good strike of the cue ball.

The player must first pocket a red ball and then try to pocket any colour, based on his choice of scoring value. He must then score another red ball before pocketing a coloured ball again. This alternation keeps going on until the remaining balls are only the coloured ones. At this point, the balls must be taken in order of increasing value, until the last one is pocketed.

Points are also scored when an opponent player commits a foul. The most common foul is failing to hit the balls in the correct order, e.g., a coloured ball after pocketing a red one. A "snooker" is a situation, in which the previous player positions the cue ball in such a manner that the correct ball can't be struck without getting obstructed by a wrong ball. Also, hitting the cue ball into a pocket is a foul.

Wall of fame

Stephen Hendry of Scotland has won 36 championships.

Ronnie O'Sullivan of England holds the record for the most ranking titles, 41.

Scottish player John Higgins is the winner of 31 titles.

Fact card

- If a player cannot hit the red/coloured ball as required, he/she forfeits his/her chance and is said to be "snookered".
- Sometimes "snooker" is also used as a derogatory term to refer to a cadet or a newbie.
- The longest game of snooker to ever be played lasted for a whopping 93 minutes and 12 seconds!
- According to research, the average age of snooker players is 35.6 years. This is more than any other sport played.

Calva

Shepherds have long been known to come up with interesting games. Some of these, like cricket, became international sports with millions of followers. A less successful one, known from Spain is Calva, which involves a steer's skull and a stone.

The calva is arranged to stand on its side and has to be knocked down.

The marro is thrown at the calva in an attempt to knock it over.

Origin

Calva is a traditional sport played in certain parts of Spain. Developed by the Celtiberians, the origin of the game is rooted back in the pre-Roman times.

It was a game for shepherds, who threw stones at the bull's horns to entertain themselves. With passing time, the game was modified; a piece of wood (the calva) came as a substitution for the horns. Further, the stone was replaced with a cylinder of iron or steel (the marro).

A man throws the marro at the calva, attempting to knock it down.

Gameplay

The objective of calva is to knock down a piece of wood, which is supported on one of its sides. The player, standing 14.5 m away from the calva, must hit it with the marro, a metal cylinder. The player has a total of 25 throws to achieve a hit, with two practice throws being provided at the beginning.

The calva is generally made of oak and has the form of an obtuse angle. It is made between 110^0 to 120^0 to resemble a bull's horn. The calva has two parts; the lower part or the zapata, which has a length of 23 cm and the upper part or the alzada, which is 22 cm long.

The marro, as it used to be in the olden days. Back then, it was a naturally occurring rock.

The marro was originally a rock taken from a creekbed. These were chosen because, the rocks used to be smooth in texture due to the stream's flow. Today, it is usually an iron cylinder or oval with the name of its owner, weight, length, etc., inscribed on it. The marro cannot be greater than 25 cm in length and generally weighs between 2 or 3 kg.

The field of play is usually about 25 m in length and about 5 m in width.

Calva is played in places like Castile and Navarre. They are both in Spain. Pamplona, the capital city of Navarre, is another hub for the practice of this sport. Calva is also played in Madrid, Barcelona, Plasencia, Biscay, Salamanca and Zamora. People from all of these places also come together to play the sport in a competitive setting. The competitions are mostly informal.

Fact card

- Calva, the horn, is derived from the word "calvaria", meaning the "skull".
- Today, the sport is practiced mainly in Castile, Salamanca, Zamora, Biscay, Madrid and Barcelona.

Pool

Pool or pocket billiards is one of the table games, which is played with a cloth-covered table. It falls into the larger billiards family.

Origin

Pool is a version of billiards, which is specifically referred to as pocket billiards. The World Pool-Billiard Association, the governing body for pool, has devised the nomenclature.

According to the Oxford English Dictionary, pool is defined as, a game played on a small billiard table using two sets of seven coloured and numbered balls together with one black ball and a white cue ball, with the aim of pocketing all one's own balls and then the black.

Gameplay

Modern pool tables generally have six pockets along the rails. There are hundreds of variations of Pool, the most common ones being:

Eight-Ball

Eight-ball is played with a full rack of 15 balls and the cue ball. Each player aims to claim a suit (commonly, stripes or solids in the USA, and reds or yellows in the UK).

He/she tries pocketing all of them and then legally pocketing the eight-ball, while destroying the opponent's opportunities to do the same. Pocketing the eight-ball early by accident forfeits the game.

A full set of pool balls before it is broken by the player who takes the first shot.

A player takes a shot at a striped ball in a game of pool.

Nine-ball

Nine-ball uses only one through nine-balls and a cue ball. It is a rotational game, in which the player must make legal contact with the lowest numbered ball on the table or a foul is called.

The game is won by legally pocketing the nine-ball. This is the most predominant game on the professional circuit.

Bank pool is another type of game played. It has been steadily gaining popularity over the years. In this format, there are nine-balls to be arranged in a nine-ball bank fashion. The game can be played with a full rank, but this will take a long time to play. The first player to "bank" five-balls in any random order is considered the winner.

Fact card

In the USA, the original game of pool was played on a pocket-less Carom Billiards table.

Carom Billiards

Most billiards games focus on pocketing the balls, mostly in the right order. Carom billiards is different in a major way that there are no pockets on the board. Here, the objective is to get the rebound angles and the strength correct.

A player taking a shot in a Carom Billiards game.

Origin

The word "carom", sometimes spelled as "carrom", means "to bounce or strike off another". It is suggested that the word is a shortened form of the Spanish word "carambola" or the French word "carambole", which were used to describe the red object ball.

Gameplay

Carom billiards is played on a table which does not have pockets. The game is played with three balls; two white balls and one red ball. One of the two white balls has a small red dot or spot to differentiate it from the second one.

One of the white balls (plain or with the spot) serves as the "cue ball", and the red ball and the remaining white ball serve as the "object balls".

The objective of the game is to strike the cue ball so that it hits the two object balls in succession, scoring a carom or billiard. This counts as one point.

The object ball has to be hit along with the red ball by the cue stick.

The cue ball is used to hit the other object balls.

Fact card

- The modern French "carambolage" refers to a car piled up in an accident, much like a ball striking other balls.
- Competition disciplines sometimes include multiple versions of the game at once, which are called "Triathlons" or "Pentathlons".

Versions

The game is played in multiple versions, some of which have become obsolete as well.

The versions are the straight rail, champion's game, balkline, cushion carom, three- cushion billiards and artistic of fantastique billiards, to name a few.

In a variety of the game, called the three-cushion billiards, the cue ball must also touch one of the cushions three or more times to complete a carom. Scoring a carom also entitles the player with another shot. His/her turn continues until he/she misses.

It is not necessary that the game be played with two white balls; one with a dot and the other without.

The game is often played with another coloured ball. In this game, the white ball is the cue ball, and the other two balls can be red and any other colour.

Carom billiards is also played in video games. In fact, all cue sports are played on the computer or the mobile phone. Even here, there is a lot of strategy and positioning to be used.

WATER SPORTS

Who doesn't enjoy playing in the water? One of the best ways to spend time in water is to swim. Swimming is also a great way to exercise the body. Swimming has also become a popular sport. There are several other activities and sports performed in the water. They are called "water sports". The buoyancy property of water allows human beings to stay afloat in the water. Water supports the human body weight. After one learns to swim and becomes comfortable in the water, they can move on to learning how to perform some of the other water sports. As more and more people got into water sports, the activities came into demand and became competitive sports.

Some water sports developed as a consequence of exploring large bodies of water. Surfing, windsurfing and wakeboarding are examples of adventure sports, which have been added to the list of water sports. Let's dive into this section to explore the different water sports played around the world.

Did you know? In water skiing, usually one boat tows one water skier. It is very impressive if two or more water skiers are towed along the same boat. In 2010, Tasmania's Horsehead Water Ski Resort set a world record when one boat towed 145 water skiers at the same time.

Swimming

Swimming is one of the most common activities. Swimming as a sport, however, is an entirely different world altogether. It involves competitive races but held in water bodies.

Origin

The earliest record of swimming dates back to the Stone Age paintings around 10,000 years ago. Some text in past manuscripts like the Gilgamesh, Iliad, Odyssey, Bible and Quran refer to swimming as an activity and exercise. Thus, we can safely say that people have been taking up swimming for many years. It has been a part of human life since the ancient times.

In the Greek and Roman Empires, young boys were trained to become soldiers and political leaders. Swimming was a compulsory part of their curriculum. It was seen as a way to shape the body and make it strong. Along with basic education and martial combat, swimming was used as training for soldiers. The ancient Assyrian, Japanese and Indian cultures also have references to swimming for training and physical development.

In the Middle Ages, fewer people took up swimming. During this time, water bodies around large settlements became heavily polluted. Frequent epidemics of water-borne diseases like cholera and jaundice broke out. As a result, people began to avoid water activities.

Swimming as a competitive sport is a fairly modern development. It began with the invention of indoor swimming pools. People began to use these pools and got back into swimming. By 1837, six indoor swimming pools were built in the city of London. It was around this time that competitive swimming came about and gained popularity.

In 1896, swimming became a part of the Olympic games. Today, the sport is regulated by the Fédération Internationale de Natation (FINA). It is conducted in indoor swimming pools. The exceptions to this are the 5 km, 10 km (included in the Olympics) and 25 km distance races, which are held in open water bodies.

Rules

The objective of swimming is to finish the race in the least time possible. The rules are quite simple. The swimmer is not supposed start before the starter's gun and shouldn't stray from his/her assigned lane. The regulations also restrict certain equipment like wearing full bodysuits. Beyond that, swimming majorly focuses on form. Swimming competitions are carried in a swimming pool that measures 50 m × 25 m.

Wall of fame

Michael Fred Phelps II is a competition swimmer from the USA. He has won 28 medals in the Olympic Games. He currently holds the all-time record for Olympic gold medals in individual events. He has been named the most successful swimmer in 2004, 2008 and 2012.

Sun Yang was the first Chinese male swimmer to win a gold medal in the Olympics. He was called "Rookie of the Year" in 2010 by the CCTV Sports Awards. In 2011, he broke the world record in the 1500-m freestyle which was previously set by Grant Hackett in 2001. It was the longest held record in any swimming competition.

Katie Ledecky, a renowned American swimmer, has won nine gold medals and 21 world championship gold medals, the most in history for a female swimmer.

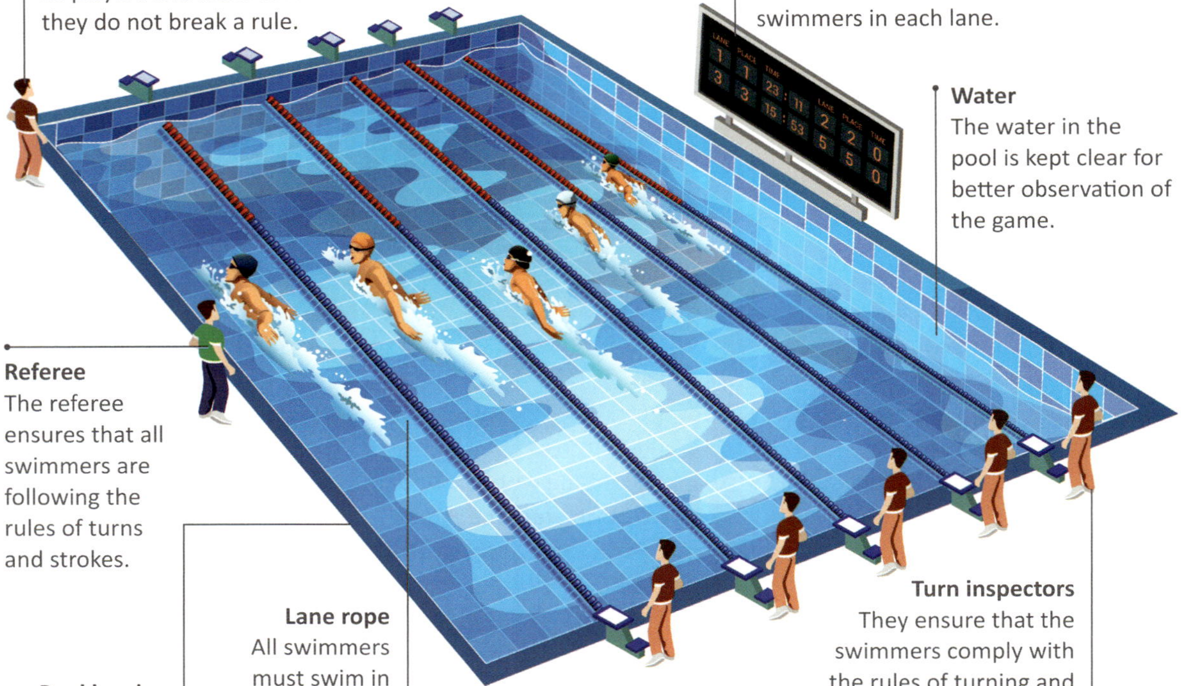

Finish judge
They inspect the finishes of all players and make sure they do not break a rule.

Score board
It displays the points awarded to the swimmers in each lane.

Water
The water in the pool is kept clear for better observation of the game.

Referee
The referee ensures that all swimmers are following the rules of turns and strokes.

Turn inspectors
They ensure that the swimmers comply with the rules of turning and report violations.

Lane rope
All swimmers must swim in their own lanes. Otherwise they will get disqualified.

Pool border
The players cannot stand near or touch this area.

There are four main swimming styles recognised today. They are:

The butterfly
This stroke is used only in competition. The stroke was brought to the attention of the US officials in 1933. Henry Myers, who used the stroke in that race, invented it. After a period of controversy, the butterfly was recognised as a distinct competitive stroke in 1953.

The backstroke
This is the only stroke that is performed on one's back. In this stroke, the swimmer's body position is supine and the body is kept as flat and streamlined as possible. The arms reach alternately above the head and enter the water directly in line with the shoulders. The palm faces outward with the little finger entering the water first. The arm is pulled back towards the thigh with a slight body roll.

Front crawl
The front crawl is the fastest of all the strokes. It is also excellently suited for long distances and choppy waters. As a result, in the freestyle event, players inevitably choose a front crawl.

Breaststroke
The breaststroke is also referred to as "the frog" due to the motion of arms involved. Breaststroke is the most popular recreational style since the swimmer's head is out of the water for a large portion of the time. Also, it can be swum comfortably at slow speeds, making it ideal for beginners.

Fact card

- Swimmers shave off all body hair to reduce drag or resistance that the body creates in water.

Sailing

Sailing has existed for hundreds of years. Sailing boats were used by explorers to travel all around the world. It slowly became an art which was practiced by prosperous people. Today, it is a major sport.

Origin

Racing boats for competitions is believed to have started in the Netherlands during the seventeenth century. The people of that time used sailboats for the races. Soon, sailing boats were customised to create "yachts", which were more ideal for racing. The Royal Yacht Squadron was established in 1815 in England. This boosted the world of boat racing. Until the invention of steam-driven vessels, yachts and sailing boats were the major vessels of transport. Even today, the term "sailboat racing" is synonymous with "yacht racing".

In 1661, John Evelyn recorded a competition between Katherine and Anne. These were the names of the sailing vessels designed by Britains. King Charles II of England owned the vessel that lost.

A sailing competition is called "regatta". It usually consists of multiple individual races to be completed by the same boat. The boat that performs best in each race is the overall winner. Sailing is regulated by the International Sailing Federation (ISAF).

RSS

The Racing Rules of Sailing (often abbreviated to RRS) has a new revision published every four years (after the Olympics). This is taken care of the International Sailing Federation (ISAF). There are many sub-sailing federations created in countries to govern national sailing bodies. The ISAF is considered the sport's world governing body. In 1997, the rules were drastically simplified from what they were in the 1940s.

Four rules of General Limitations:

- If a boat has a right-of-way, it is considered their duty to avoid collision. If the other boat is not keeping clear, the boat with the right-of-way must keep clear.
- If one boat acquires the right-of-way, the other boat must be given the room first to keep clear.
- A boat that changes course even if it has the right-of-way, shall do so in a manner that gives the burdened boat a chance to "keep clear".
- If a boat catches up with another which wants to pass it and take the leeward track, the first boat should not luff higher than one would have done if that boat wasn't there.

There are also three rules of marks and obstructions, three other rules about starting errors, taking penalties, moving astern and finally, three rules about interfering with another boat.

Cutter boats are small or medium-sized. They are designed for speed. They have less capacity.

Four right of way rules:

- Boats moving on a port tack must steer clear of boats on a starboard tack.
- If two boats run on the same track and overlap, the windward boat must steer clear of the leeward boat.
- If two boats are on the same track but do not overlap, the boat that is astern must keep clear of the boat ahead.
- If a boat is tacking (changing tracks), it should keep clear of the ones not tacking.

Wall of fame

The Windjammer Parade is the world's biggest regatta and sailing event which is held in Germany.

The Sydney to Hobart Yacht Race is a yearly event hosted by the Cruising Yacht Club of Australia. It starts in Sydney.

The Fastnet Race is a biennial offshore yachting race held in the United Kingdom. It is organised by the Royal Ocean Racing Club.

The Bermuda Race is a biennial sailing yacht race which goes from Newport, Rhode Island, to the island of Bermuda.

Fact card

- In sailing competitions, paths or courses are marked by buoys in the ocean.
- The wind that a boat experiences is the combination of "true wind" which is natural wind and the wind created by the forward movement of the boat.
- Wind shear affects the moving sailboats when the direction of the wind changes at different wind speeds.
- Sailing boats with one hull are called "monohulls" and those with two are called "catamarans".

Synchronised Swimming

This is a floating formation performed by the group of synchronised swimmers.

Most Olympic sports are judged on the basis of strength, endurance, speed or skill. Synchronised swimming is a notable exception to this as it closely resembles a dance or art form, and is judged accordingly.

Origin

Synchronised swimming was earlier referred to as "water ballet" because of the grace and beauty involved in the movements made by the participants. The term "synchronised swimming" was coined by Norman Ross. It came about at the turn of the twentieth century. The first recorded competition was held in 1891 in Berlin, Germany. The competitions were mainly conducted in indoor pools, like in the case of swimming competitions. As people quickly began to appreciate it as an art form, synchronised swimming competitions were also held in the theatres of London and Glasgow. These theatres were equipped with huge on-stage water tanks built especially for these competitions.

Synchronised swimming gained popularity among the masses in1907, when an Australian swimmer, Annette Kellerman, delivered a performance inside a glass tank. She performed as an underwater ballerina in the New York Hippodrome. This performance fascinated the viewers. Word of this wonderful performance quickly spread.

In this sport, the execution of strokes, "tricks" and floating formations are a major must. The formation of the first Water Ballet club brought about the invention of these tricks and strokes. The club was formed in Chicago by Katherine Curtis. On 27th May, 1939, the USA held its first synchronised swimming competition at Wright Junior College in Chicago. It was not until 1968 that this sport became officially recognised by FINA as the fourth water sport after swimming, diving and water polo. After Curtis' death in 1980, synchronised swimming became an official Olympics sport in the 1984 Summer Olympic Games.

Synchronised swimmers wear beautiful and elaborate costumes, just like regular ballet performers.

Rules

Synchronised swimming is judged on the basis of grace and co-ordination.

Some routines are preset and compulsory, while the competitors can add on some other routines to impress the judges.

A standard meet begins with the swimmers doing "figures". These are progressions between positions performed individually without music.

Synchronised swimming competitions can be performed solo, as a duet or in groups.

Earlier, synchronised swimmers had to wear a compulsory costume of a black swimsuit and white swim cap, along with a pair of goggles and a nose clip. Today, there is more freedom in the costumes, but certain rules still apply. Costumes are more elaborate and are designed with the performance in mind. Figures are performed in front of a panel of five judges, who score individual swimmers from one to 10 (10 being the highest).

The figure competition prefaces the routine events. During a routine, swimmers are not allowed to use the bottom of the pool for support. Instead they rely upon sculling motions with the arms and "eggbeater kicks" to keep themselves afloat. After the performance, the swimmers are judged and scored on their performance based on technical merit and artistic impression. Technical scores account for 50 per cent of the total score, whereas artistic expressions or free routine performances account for the remaining 50 per cent.

Judges keep a close eye on the position of the hands and arms.

If any swimmer holds hands loosely, it results in a negative score.

Duet competitions were restored during the 2000 Olympics.

Wall of fame

Annette Marie Sarah Kellermann was not only a professional swimmer but also a film actress, writer and business woman. Though she put synchronised swimming on the map with her performance, she was not a professional synchronised swimmer.

Natalia Sergeyenva Ischenko is a Russian competitor and a triple Olympic gold medallist. She has competed in solo and women's duet performances. She took a break in 2013 after her pregnancy and returned to the competition world in 2015, during which time she won the duet and team events in the Synchro Cup.

Fact card

- Swimmers use nose clips to prevent water from entering their noses during the underwater routines.
- Swimmers use extensive eye makeup to portray emotions. The makeup they wear is waterproof. The use of it has been a matter of heavy criticism among purists.
- Synchronised swimming is a female-dominated sport as men are barred from the Olympics.
- Esther Williams popularised synchronised swimming during World War II.

Diving

Diving is a sport which begins with a leap in the air using the diving board and ends with a spring into the water. Those who perform dives for competitions are called "divers". It is a challenging and beautiful sport.

Origin

The first record of competitive diving was in 1889 during the Championships of Scotland. Diving was not as complex in this event. The participants dove into the water from the side of a bath. Later, a six-foot dive and a surface dive were introduced in these competitions. Diving was included in the Olympic Games in 1904. In 1908, it became a part of the springboard and platform events during the Olympic Games in London. Women began to participate in the diving event from the 1912 Olympic Games, which were held in Stockholm.

High dive was introduced in the later 1800s. Fancy dives were introduced to the world of sport diving in 1903. In 1904, springboard diving was included in the Olympic Games. High diving was included as a supplementary activity in the Athens Olympic Games in 1906. By 1924, participants used six methods of performing dives in the Olympics. These are standing, running, taking off with one foot and running taking off with two feet are some examples. Divers are scored on their starting position, approach, takeoff, flight and entry. Each of these components of the dive score a maximum of three points.

Springboard diving is the most popular form of diving.

Fact card

- Competitors must have a Confédération Mondiale des Activités Subaquatiques (CMAS) diving certificate to participate in competitions.
- While most think that diving is a sport that creates a lot of splash, divers are given extra points by the judges when they create little or no splash.

This diver is performing a high dive with a hurdle at the end before the sprint.

Tournaments

The following is a list of major tournaments that have taken place so far in the sport of diving:

- First European Sport Diving Championship
- Second Sport Diving World Cup
- Snow Fins 2012 – CMAS International Finswimming and Sport Diving Competition
- Second European Sport Diving Championship
- First World Championship

Rules

In major diving competitions, the divers compete for the 3 m springboard and the 10 m platform. The divers can perform voluntary or optional dives. They need to produce a dive list sheet to the director before the competition.

While taking the approach step, the divers must keep their body steady with their arms straight and to the side. They must walk three steps forward with a hurdle at the last step if they plan to take a forward approach. If they balk, the judges deduct the points.

In case a diver wants to perform a flight step, he/she must keep legs together.

Water Polo

Water polo is a combination sport of volleyball and swimming. There are also elements of football and basketball mixed into the game.

Origin

By the late nineteenth century, water sports became an inseparable feature of county fairs and festivals in many parts of England and Scotland. One of the earliest recorded antecedents of the modern game of water polo was a game of water handball played at Bournemouth on 13th July, 1876. Water polo began as a demonstration of one's skills in swimming and strength.

The game came to be called "water polo" because the Baltic people called ball "pulu" and pronounced it as "polo". Water polo has been a part of the Olympic Games since the 1900s. Today, water polo is played all over the world. It is especially popular in Europe and North America.

Goalkeepers can touch and catch the ball with both their hands. They can hit it with their fist.

The goalkeeper defends the goalpost and makes sure that the attacking team does not make a goal.

Gameplay

Each team has 13 players with six field players, seven in the pool and a goalie. The attacking team controls the ball and tries to score. The defending team tries to get the ball and block any attempts to score. Once the defending team gets the ball, they become the attackers.

A game has four periods. Each period has a duration of eight minutes. At the start of each period, the teams must line up along the goal line and remain there until the referee signals the start of the game.

A goal is made when the ball crosses the goal line within the goal posts. Carrying is allowed and so is shooting the ball for the purpose of scoring a goal.

A player can catch and throw the ball with the intention of passing it to another player.

Water polo players wear protective headgear and shorts.

Hungary, Italy and the Great Britain (in that order) are the top three countries in the field of water polo. They are ranked according to the number of Olympic gold medals they have won. Hungary has won nine gold medals, while Italy and the Great Britain have won four each. Italy has also won two silver medals.

Fact card

- Water polo is a violent game and players are often suspended for committing exclusion fouls like pulling back a player or splashing water in an opponent's face.

Biribol

Biribol is a mix of water polo and volleyball. It is a highly competitive sport which is gaining popularity in Brazil. It is named "Biribol" after the city of "Birigul" in Brazil, where the sport was invented.

Origin

Dario Miguel Pedro created the game as a group sport to provide an alternative to his students who wanted to steer from swimming practice and lessons.

The net is placed in the middle of the pool. The size and height of the net is dependant upon if the team is made up of male players or female players.

Gameplay

Biribol is played in indoor pools that are 8 m long, 4 m wide and half m in depth, without any slope.

Each game has three sets. Each set is scored in 21 points. The team which wins two out of three sets wins the game. A team needs a two-point advantage to win the set or game. In the event of a tie, the match is extended to two more points.

Players can touch the ball with their hands (open or closed) or with their bodies.

The Biribol game traditionally has four players in each team. There is also a doubles system.

Ball

In this game, the inside part of the pool is considered neutral. So, once the ball is thrown into the pool, it is anybody's game. The ball must stay in the air. If the ball touches the water in the opponent's side, they get a point. If the opponent team commits a fault, a point is scored. Before the ball crosses the net, the team can have contact three times and not more than that.

A player cannot make contact with the ball twice. It needs to be made by three different players. It is only in the case of blocking where double contact by the same person is not counted. Players lose a point for the team if they touch the net. Opponent layers can block serves as they are being made.

Popularity

Biribol is an extremely competitive sport. It is highly popular in Brazil, but not so in other countries. Brazil has several national leagues of its own. It is an official sport in the state of Sao Paulo, where most players hail from.

The ball in biribol is similar to the ball in the water polo game.

Fact card

- Biribol is a genuinely Brazilian game from start to finish.

Windsurfing

Surfers have been known to travel the world in search of the perfect wave. However, windsurfing is for those surfers who are more interested in the sport itself rather than the wave. Windsurfing is a combination sport which combines surfing and sailing. It is an adventure sport.

In windsurfing competitions, players try as best as they can to adhere to one track and avoid injuries.

Origin

Sailing boats have been in existence for thousands of years. Ancient Polynesian pieces of art depict men riding large waves in the oceans. These men are standing upright on a solid board with a vertical sail. These paintings either suggest that windsurfing was probably in existence even back then, or that the idea of windsurfing appealed to people.

Sails make use of the wind to move forward. There is a lot of complex activity involved in trying to steer the boat in the required direction while keeping the speed in control. The same is applied to windsurfing.

However the modern version of Windsurfing emerged only in the late twentieth century. Newman Darby was 21 years old at the time. He was the first person to use a handheld sail and rig which was mounted on a universal joint. He controlled his small catamaran using the sail and rig. This was in 1948, but it wasn't until 16 years later, in 1964, that Darby began selling his sailboards. On 27th March, 1968, Hoyle Schweitzer and Jim Drake filed the very first windsurfing patent. Sailboarding or windsurfing has been an Olympics sport since 1984. Women were allowed to participate from 1992.

Rules

Freestyle windsurfing is judged on the basis of style and creativity. Racing windsurfing involves running a course in the least possible time. Standard Olympic rules apply for this style.

Racing longboards are used in the Olympic racing competitions. Beginner boards are smaller and are used for learners.

The windsurfer tilts the rig and carves the board to perform a move called "carve".

Windsurfers hold on to the rig. Their feet are strapped to the board.

A windsurfer enjoys the declining wave.

Fact card

- Experienced sailors have been able to reach speeds of over 40 knots using specialised equipment.

Aquathlon

There are many sports, which combine a variety of disciplines to test a gamut of an athlete's skills. An interesting duo of these is racing and swimming, forming the sport of aquathlons.

Aquathlons were inspired from triathlons. But triathlons have land races like running, hurdles and other such events.

Origin

Aquathlons have been around for a long time. They were conducted for ocean lifeguard competitions. Since the early twentieth century, the competitions increased in number and popularity. The objective of the aquathlons is to rescue a person or doll from a trapped box. These are kept in one section of the water. The participants have to race to that section and overcome several obstacles on the way. Speed, time and endurance along with quick wit are a must for these competitions.

The National Surf Lifesaving Association of America was formed in 1965. In its inaugural year, the NSLAA held its first national competition, in which one of the events was called "run-swim-run".

The modern aquathlons follow the system of a 400 m run – 400 m swim – 200 m run.

Gameplay

Most events in an aquathlon are open-water events. Some of them also include sprints or super sprints. The latter are held in indoor pools or in a more controlled area.

The various course lengths are:

Warm water: Two and a half km run – one km swim – two and a half km run

Cold water (below 22° C): 1 km swim (the participant must wear a mandatory wetsuit) – 5 km run. Long courses directly double each of the distances.

Before an aquathlon, participants make sure to get a lot of running and swimming practice. Running in the water is tougher than running on land as there is more resistance.

Federations

- The sport is governed and sanctioned by the International Triathlon Union. There are various federations under it, which are active to various degrees.
- The British Triathlon Federation (BTF) trains athletes and holds events in cold water conditions (around 12°C).
- The Icelandic Triathlon Federation hosts even colder aquathlons (around 10°C).

Participants need to be comfortable in such settings.

Fact card

- A similar event to aquathlon called the "duathlon" exists. It replaces the swimming leg with a cycling event.